you

only

live

once

kendra leonard

BALBOA.PRESS
A DIVISION OF HAY HOUSE

Balboa Press books may be ordered through booksellers or by contacting:

Balboa Press
A Division of Hay House
1663 Liberty Drive
Bloomington, IN 47403
www.balboapress.com
844-682-1282

Because of the dynamic nature of the Internet, any web addresses or
links contained in this book may have changed since publication and
may no longer be valid. The views expressed in this work are solely those
of the author and do not necessarily reflect the views of the publisher,
and the publisher hereby disclaims any responsibility for them.

The author of this book does not dispense medical advice or prescribe the
use of any technique as a form of treatment for physical, emotional, or medical
problems without the advice of a physician, either directly or indirectly. The
intent of the author is only to offer information of a general nature to help you
in your quest for emotional and spiritual well-being. In the event you use any
of the information in this book for yourself, which is your constitutional right,
the author and the publisher assume no responsibility for your actions.

Any people depicted in stock imagery provided by Getty Images are
models, and such images are being used for illustrative purposes only.
Certain stock imagery © Getty Images.

Print information available on the last page.

ISBN: 978-1-9822-7246-3 (sc)
ISBN: 978-1-9822-7247-0 (e)

Balboa Press rev. date: 06/26/2023

for

my daughter

my family

my friends

my lover

my associates

my clients

myself

Contents

in the beginning

i always tell people i lived life backwards...

so when i was twenty, i found out i was pregnant. two weeks later i found out i was having twins. two weeks after that, i found out i had shed one out. i was left with a two vessel umbilical cord, instead of three. and the doctors told me that my unborn child had a 30% higher chance of having chromosomal abnormalities. due to these complications, and breaking a rule of my father's by actually getting pregnant, i finished my sophomore year at nc state university and put my college education on hold.

i loved being pregnant. of course that means that i experienced no sickness or swelling, other than gaining exactly 40 pounds that evenly distributed on top of my 97 pounds pre-pregnant body. i felt great, i was told i had a glow about me, i ate better, and i loved being able to show off my belly as i grew. not physically, as no one should do that regardless of being pregnant or not at any age, but through my clothing. i always used clothing to express how i felt and how cool it was to have this new body to dress. although i can tell you that matte jersey left my life after pregnancy. never again…

after having ultrasounds every other week after my 7 month, and 26 hours of labor that ended with a cesarean section, my daughter, kayla, was born happy and completely healthy. healthy she was, healthy my relationship with her father was not. so it was within the first year of her life that i realized what i was willing to put myself through, not willing to put her through. i had been with my daughter's father for seven years, age 14-21. you know, the whole good girl, bad boy syndrome. somehow i managed to go from the pre-med path to a premature learning life experience. a volatile relationship, emotionally and mentally draining, but ultimately one that produced a beautiful child, which is the best thing that's ever happened to me.

being a single mother had its challenges, but i would not have had it happen any other way. kayla was completely at peace with the world. as an infant, she never cried. when there was the slightest whimper, you knew it was because she was hungry, wet, uncomfortable, or just needed some good tlc. i think i'd be pissed, too, if i crapped my pants… and just when i thought i couldn't change another diaper, she was potty trained. oh, funny story- this was my bad mommy moment-

so when kayla was potty training, i was the stockroom supervisor at banana republic. i got up around 4:30am to get her off to her home daycare, then made my way to work at 5:30am. getting off at 2:30pm was wonderful and everyone always used to say, "well, at least you can go home and take a nap." ha. clearly they didn't have a toddler. there was never naptime for me. i was completely exhausted on the regular. the second i sat down to play, i'd fall fast asleep. that's why we were always on the go- to parks, museums, nature walks, etc. well, one night after waking up at the crack of dawn and working, then playing all day, we started our nighttime routine. this consisted of a bath, brushing miniature teeth, story time, song time, then prayers followed by a goodnight hug and kiss of course.

well, after all that, kayla told me she had to go to the bathroom. if you didn't know, when your child who's potty training tells you they have to go, you go. well, she didn't. she sat and waited, and nothing came. so we went back to bed, more hugs and kisses and she says she has to go again. so of course, we rush back to the bathroom and nothing. i ran the water, nothing. finally we went back to her room again to say goodnight. now mind you, by this time it's about 9pm. needless to say, i am pooped. we then have one more round of going to the bathroom. at this point, i told kayla to sit and try again, and to come and get me when she was done. i took her pull up and her pants with me and went to lay down. bad idea.

next thing i knew, i woke up to the sound of laughter. the laughter was coming from my best friend who lived with us at the time. she and her boyfriend had just come home after being out and about. she waved me off and told me to go back to bed and that she'd explain in the morning. it was at this time that i realized that i still had kayla's pull up and pants in my possession. my friend proceeded to tell me what happened...

so she and her boyfriend pulled up to the house and noticed that each and every one of the lights were on. upon entering, they saw kayla in the living room. she had her night shirt on, absolutely nothing on her lower half except one sock pulled all the way up to her knee. she had the other sock in her hand and when they came inside she exclaimed "mommy's sleeping! mommy's sleeping!" while she waved the sock in the air and turned in circles. glad i passed my dancing gene onto my child- i can only imagine the sight. apparently my child decided to turn on every light in the house and have a half-naked dance party. it was from that night on, that i sat with bloodshot eyes patiently waiting for kayla to finish her business in the bathroom instead of laying down on the job.

as a toddler, i remembered how everyone warned me about the terrible two's. i had no idea what they were referring to. kayla was perfect. then two and a half came. holy shit. i remember she had one melt down. we were in target and she wanted something that i wasn't going to get for her. she became demon possessed, almost did a back flop onto the floor in the middle of the isle, and kicked and screamed like an upside down cockroach. i was stunned. i came to the conclusion that the main reason toddlers have these breakdowns is because they do not have the vocabulary to express their emotions. if you can't tell from reading this so far, i'm a talker. so that's what i did with her. "i understand you're upset that you can't have that toy," etc. same thing leaving the playground. you give them a heads up- "we're leaving in fifteen minutes," "okay, just another ten more minutes," "you only have five minutes left to play." imagine if you were immediately yanked out of whatever it was that you were doing... makes sense, right?

anyway, kayla and i did everything together. we routinely went to the zoo, to the beach, volunteered for charity, went to the ballet. she was my best little friend in the whole wide world. just like i loved being pregnant, i adored being a mother. i was very involved in the classroom, always a room parent, wanting to spend every moment i could with her. when i was with her, i was all mommy. kendra time would have to come every other weekend when she was with her father. that was my time to dance the night away and spend time with friends.

just the two of us + one

for the first four years of her life, it was just the two of us. it was on
her fourth birthday that we actually added someone else to our family,
my boyfriend, miguel. he was a client of mine at banana republic, and
the only man i had ever gotten tongue tied over besides kayla's father.
he used to come into the store and my tongue would literally unravel
onto the floor. everyone on staff asked me who he was cause i can
talk to anyone, but when he came in i got all sheepish and shy. after
being harassed by my associates, i finally got the nerve to ask him
out. i suggested we go out for coffee sometime and he said, "well,"
and i responded with "of course, you must have a girlfriend, " and
he said "well," it was at this time that i realized that he was actually
married. even though i'm addicted to clothing, i don't consider myself
materialistic (i know that's a complete contradiction, but that's who i
am, a pisces- a fish swimming in opposite directions). i never noticed
that he wore a wedding ring. oops...

i felt like an ass. i apologized and he started to say that things weren't so great, but i stopped him there and said that i did not want to be any source of temptation for him. ever since then, he would come in and i could speak like an intelligent human being again. the first time i said 'hello' after that he questioned that i was still going to speak to him? i said,"of course, but i'm just not going to ask you out for coffee." well a year and a half went by and he had disclosed that he was going through a separation. it was one saturday, about four years after we first met, that he called me at the store. he said he didn't know how to get in contact with me otherwise, but wanted to ask me to go to lunch. it was at this moment that i asked to put him on hold so i could jump up and down and scream like a little girl. i returned to the phone and accepted his offer. we went to lunch the very next day, talked for four hours, and after four months of courting me daily, at the end of my daughter's fourth year of life, we moved in together.

i had been at banana republic for several years doing everything from merchandising, scheduling, auditing, hiring, training, and anything and everything dealing with the internal and external clients. one of my many roles at banana republic was to be the store community leader. it was my job to come up with creative ways to give back to the community. i decided what better way to raise money for non-profits than by having quarterly fashion shows. we sold tickets for $10, held a silent auction, and had our employees as the models. the first show raised $500. initially, we started raising money for habitat for humanity. we ended up raising enough money to build a house, so we did. if you ever do this, know that it is so worth it, just beware of tar- don't sit in it. not a pretty (or comfortable) site…

we then focused our efforts on the alliance of aids services carolinas for a while. we organized our teams and did the aids walk two years in a row, and continued doing quarterly fashion shows to raise money as well. this was when the whole [red] campaign at gap, inc. got started. another perfect fit. it was after our summer charity fashion show that i just happened to stay late at work (which i tried to never do) and one of my associates came in early. we just rarely saw each other. well, she asked if i knew that the owner of the salon who did our hair and make up for the shows, her son had leukemia. i had no clue, and she suggested maybe switching organizations like we had in the past. well, it was that night that i went home that miguel told me had been diagnosed with leukemia.

miguel was a super health nut. we had a gym in our house, he worked out six days a week religiously. he was the guy who documented how fast he ran, how far he ran, how much he benched, etc. after three days of feeling dizzy and getting fevers after his workouts, he decided to go to urgent care to get checked out. they tested his blood four times because they thought the machine was broken. the doctor actually tested her blood just in case, because clearly, a man with 60,000 white blood cells in his system (normally we have 3,000-7,000) should not be standing in front of them like nothing is devastatingly wrong. it was at this time that they told miguel that he most likely had leukemia and that he needed to go to the cancer center the next day for testing.

this same day was also the last day of classes for me, as i had gone back to school on a part time basis over three years to finish my degree since i had not earned my undergraduate degree yet. it was my mission to finish my degree and pursue a career in pharmaceutical sales. this concept actually came at the suggestion of five clients of mine over the years at banana republic. and after looking into the specifics, i knew that this position was made for me. with my fascination of anatomy and physiology coupled with psychology and the environment, i had found my niche. so finishing school was my ticket to leave banana republic and retail altogether. so prior to hearing this news i thought 'finally, one less thing on my plate.' not so much...

well, the next day i had already set up a meeting with glaxosmithkline. miguel strongly suggested that i keep it and go as this is the reason why i went back to school, the meeting i had been waiting for three years. we had an informal interview, and the representative actually said that 'i looked kinda rough,' but i knew it would be unprofessional to say anything to him at this time. the meeting went well and he told me he would speak with his district manager to schedule a ride along as the next step to see how i did in the field. i went from that meeting to the cancer center with miguel. he was actually misdiagnosed with having acute myelogenous leukemia and was told he had a week to wrap up work and things before he started his treatment. because of his health and his age, the doctors were very optimistic.

at miguel's request i also went to work the next day. he said it would be a good distraction and we needed to save my time off for when it was really necessary. i normally walk around at 100 mph with a massive smile on my face, interacting with clients and my staff. i was a complete mess that day. the second anyone looked at me and asked me what was wrong, i broke down into tears. my first client that saw me in this state enlightened me that i must have been prepared to handle this type of battle based on the things that i had gone through in my life. that's when it dawned on me why i must have gone through hell and back with kayla's father. epiphany.

i'm sorry, what?!

however, i was about to enter a new side of hell. when we came back
on monday for a biopsy, miguel's 60,000 cells doubled to 120,000. they
told us to go home and pack a bag and get to the hospital immediately.
his disease was more aggressive than they thought and he needed
to start chemotherapy as soon as possible. having already been in
a zombi like state, we headed into another worldwind. when we got
to the hospital, we went through the admissions process. when they
asked miguel if i was his wife, he grabbed my hand and said that i was
his girlfriend, his life partner. after going through the process, he was
given a room and the poking and prodding began. they immediately
inserted a portacatheder into his chest, mainly because of the amount
of blood and drugs that was going to be given and taken throughout
this process.

he started his treatment, but it didn't even phase him. he was still running four miles on the treadmill daily like it was nothing. miguel was officially diagnosed with chronic myelogenous leukemia, but with a blast crisis. meaning he had it for some time and because it was left alone, it spun out of control and started replicating at an advanced rate. but again, doctors were optimistic. with chemotherapy, radiation, and eventually a bone marrow transplant, we had hope. after five weeks of chemo at rex, he was able to come home and take a magic pill called gleevac.

during his five weeks at home, miguel and i discussed the possibility of marriage. we were never going to get married. he was married for 14 years and was devastated when it ended in divorce. he never wanted to go through that again. it didn't really matter to me, as long as we were together, that's all i cared about. however, with the severity of the situation, and after consulting with his uncle who was a medical doctor, he told me loved me and that he would have asked me eventually, he was just scared. then he asked when my next day off was. i said 'tuesday?' we were just going to go to the courthouse when i said i needed just a teeny- tiny bit of romance, so we decided to have a super small ceremony with kayla, my mother, his best friend/photographer, our dear friends and wonderful neighbors as witnesses, and our pastor.

we decided that once he was well again that we would have a party for all of our friends and family, but right now, simplicity was all we needed. there were no rings or special dress or tux, just us and it was perfect. we drove around the corner to a gazebo on the backside of our neighborhood, and just as the pastor was about to speak, we saw the sheet of rain work its way across the pond. we quickly went back to our house and upon arrival, the sun came out, birds started chirping, and the rain was no more. we ended up getting married in our living room. it was simple sweet, and serene. after the ceremony was over, kayla performed her own version for us on our front porch with rings she had cause she couldn't believe we missed that part. so cute.

so after taking gleevac which had an 85% cure rate for his type of cancer, for another five weeks and undergoing outpatient chemotherapy, he was admitted to duke for his bone marrow transplant. on the day he was admitted to the hospital, he was given a heavy dose of radiation coupled with chemotherapy. while we were waiting for the doctor to do his rounds, i made a quick call to work to let them know i'd be a few minutes late as i did not want to leave without speaking to the doctor. i was informed at that time that i had a meeting at work and i needed to get in asap. this was completely sprung on me and i was given a hard time that i was running behind. i could not believe the lack of compassion. on the day my husband was going in for a bone marrow transplant, no less. anyway, the doctor came and explained everything and since i could not be with him during the treatment, i went to work.

when i got to work, i was brought into the office and the door shut behind me. i was bombarded by my boss and co-worker who decided that this was a great day to tell me that if i could not resolve the problems the three of us were having at work, that maybe when i was absent for the month following miguel's bone marrow transplant, that they would just realize it was better without me there in the first place. i was blown away. not only was i consumed with thoughts of whether or not my husband may or may not die of cancer, but now my job was in jeopardy?! directly after the meeting i called my district manager as well as my human resource manager, and explained what had happened. they both reassured me that i had nothing to worry about and to not concern myself with anything except my husband's health. easier said than done. talk about stress...

when i went back to the hospital after work, miguel was sleeping. he was given heavy doses of chemotherapy and radiation and for the first time, i saw my husband in a completely different way than i ever had before. he looked sick, he got sick, he was weak, it was awful. until now the 'scary' physical things had never surfaced. miguel always was slim and he always shaved his head, so that dramatic event never took place. watching my macho man husband transform into a helpless human being was a hard pill for me to swallow. fortunately his sister and brother were there to help support me during this hard time.

his brother was 100% match on all the 12 phases of typing, which is what you want so as to eliminate getting graft versus host disease. the doctors had given him medication to make his cells grow at an exponential rate. basically, our cells are grown inside our bones, called our bone marrow. once this drug took effect, the cells got so crowded inside the bone, that they escaped into the blood stream. so basically it was like a blood transfusion. it used to be that bone marrow transplants were incredibly painful, a hollow needle going into your hip and extracting the marrow. now, not so much. immediately following his bone marrow transplant, miguel had to be put on a feeding tube. slowly, he regained his strength and his cell count started to rise. within another five weeks, miguel was discharged and we relocated to an apartment in durham to be within close proximity of the hospital.

the timing could not have been better. the day he was discharged, kayla tracked out of school. so the three of us packed up and relocated into a two bedroom apartment. kayla was super involved in the process of his recovery, too. she helped sort his pills, flushed his line for his feeding tube, and over all, just supported us both during that time. after five long weeks, the doctors said that miguel was in good enough health to move back home. in october he started working out again and even kayla and i were struggling to keep up with him. he started going out again and visiting with friends on a regular basis. things seemed to be getting back to a somewhat normal place.

it was in the middle of november that we had our holiday fashion show. i was so excited, we raised over $10,000, the most we had ever raised. since our fashion show was on a sunday night, he was sleeping when i got home. he was still sleeping when i trotted off to work the next day, too, so by the time i came home to tell him, i was ecstatic to share the news. i opened my mouth to tell him, but instead he spoke first. he said his doctor called, his cancer came back, it mutated twice, and one of the mutations was not curable. my good feeling was gone. going from such an extreme high to devastating low, i was completely beside myself.

cancer sucks

this happened right after his 39th birthday and kicked off our holiday season. we had a difficult time being thankful. we headed into the hustle bustle, and on christmas day he didn't get out of bed. balancing out the holiday with my eight year old child and being by my sick husband's bedside was difficult on all of us. the day after, kayla went to her father's and we went to the hospital. they pulled me into a separate room and told me that miguel wouldn't make it through winter. i could not believe my ears. i was shocked, we're talking time frames? he started working out again, he just had one really bad day. miguel was once again admitted to the hospital for more testing. that night miguel asked what they told me. i just said, 'the same thing they told you.' he asked specifically what they said. thinking that i was delivering this information a second time to him, i just came out and said it. it was at that time that i realized that the doctors really didn't tell him the same thing at all.

had i known that i was sharing this information for the first time, i would have said it a different way. i could not believe that they told me one thing and did another. miguel was furious. it was like i was taking away his hope. i felt awful. four days later he was discharged. when we left the hospital we went straight to the funeral home to make final arrangements. again, another zombie like stage. planning your own funeral was not something he had ever thought he would have to do. we went from there to an attorney to draft his final living will. it seemed like the minutes were like hours, but everything was a blur. new years came. as everyone was celebrating a new year, we were wondering if this one would be his last.

but miguel was such a fighter. he said, "what's next? let's look into clinical trials." and that's what we did. he was accepted into a clinical trial at md anderson in houston, texas. so, at the end of january we drove across the country so his new treatment could begin. he was the first human to be on this particular clinical trial-exciting, but terrifying at the same time. family friends were so gracious in letting him stay at their home as he was undergoing treatment there. to his request, i continued working and staying at home with kayla in raleigh. he told me some day he'd need me, but he could manage on his own for now. he also told me to think of this as a long business trip. because if he didn't do this, then he was done. we remembered skype a few weeks after, and that helped make things a little easier while we were separated at this time.

i flew back and forth and a few weeks before i came to see him in march, he said he was just too tired to skype. he warned me the day before i came to see him that he looked and moved like a 90 year old man. his warning did not prepare me for what i saw. when i came to visit, not only was he crippled and twenty pounds lighter, but he was grey. he could barely walk. i believe he was already dying from the inside out at this time. upon my arrival into houston, he writhed with pain throughout the entire car ride to see his brother in dallas. the pain continued into the night and at 6:30 in the morning, i said we had to get him back into the hospital. he was put on so much pain medication that he was hallucinating constantly. the doctors said he needed a care giver 100% of the time, but miguel refused.

he forced me to get back on my plane and return home. later that week, i celebrated my 30th birthday. i remember working, no one knew, so no one wished. my boss actually snapped at me that day which just added to my self-pity. right before i left he did realize that it was my birthday and profusely apologized, so that helped. after work i met my mother and daughter for dinner. my salad was already there waiting for me. however at my fifth bite in, my entrée was delivered. i lost it. i know that sounds stupid, but miguel and i used to enjoy long dinners and the fact that i was brought my dinner before my salad was finished was a tipping point for me. it's always the small things that make a difference. i rushed to the bathroom and tears came flowing out. once i got myself together, i came out and told kayla and my mother to finish their dinner, but i needed some time alone. i drove home and balled my eyes out. i was just so exhausted emotionally.

the next week miguel was put on another clinical trial. things started turning around. he began gaining his color back and his appetite. he actually ended up gaining about 50 pounds. he continued on this path, his counts were going down, we were hoping this would be it. in the meantime, though, he told me that he was at peace, that he was okay with things. that made the world of difference. when i visited over the next few months his health seemed to improve. however in may, things started to change for the worse and he was put on another clinical trial. he also decided that he had had enough and wanted to come home. i was so grateful. this whole time i had argued as to why he couldn't be at home popping pills. so, i flew out and we drove back across the country. the summer came and went. he was slowing down and began to withdrawal from the world a little more each day.

i remember coming home from work one day and he was making rice pudding- a very common thing for him to do before all of this happened. sweat was pouring out of his head and he was having difficulty stirring the pot. i offered to help and he got angry. saying that if he couldn't even do this what was he capable of doing? it was also around this time that he tried shaving his head- again, a very common activity for him to do on a regular basis. he wasn't even half way done before he was completely exhausted. this was the last time he shaved his head. one night, close to midnight at the end of

15

september, he went into a pain crisis. we quickly gathered our things and headed for the hospital.

here we were again. it was not a good feeling of familiarity. it had been so long since we had been in this hospital. it was also taking forever for them to get us admitted. finally, a gentleman from admissions noticed miguel's pain and frustration and took it upon himself to wheel him up to 9200, a place within duke university hospital we hoped to never be in again. in fact, the staff throughout his entire experience was purely delightful. from rex, to duke, to md anderson, the special people who took care of him could not be described as anything else but angels. it was also a small team of people at duke that finally had it in their hearts to recommend hospice. it took them about a week to get the pain under control and he was just not leading a quality life. we were discharged on a thursday.

hospice came to our house on friday afternoon to explain everything. he said he was pretty sure, but wanted to have the weekend to think about it. on saturday he woke up and looked at his 42 pills and said 'i don't want to do this anymore.' on sunday he woke up and said 'oh shit. maybe i should have taken some of those.' on monday, he said he was ready. i remember thinking the first and second day that i wasn't doing enough. but by wednesday, i was completely exhausted- emotionally, mentally, and physically. because it was also at this time that kayla's father, along his mother, were attempting to take kayla away from me. according to the recommendations of the social psychologists, kayla was mature enough to make her own decision about whether she wanted to be at home with us during this time or not. their standpoint was that everything else was spiraling out of control in her life, so she should be allowed to make this one decision. her father did not agree with this way of thinking.

i let him have the conversation with kayla, that way he didn't feel like i was swaying her in a certain direction. so apparently he did give her a choice as to where she wanted to be- at home with us, with him and his girlfriend, his mother, or my mother. this conversation happened on that sunday and he called me back and said she was staying with him. i said that was fine. however, when i went to have lunch with her the next day at school, she asked why she wasn't allowed to come home. i told her that she could be wherever she'd like to be and her father should have made that clear. she said it was explained to her that way, but when she said she wanted to come home, that he said no, that she had to stay with him. so that's when i told her that i would pick her up and she could definitely come home and not to worry. she already had enough stress in her life as an 8 year old child.

i called to let both her father and his mother know that kayla wanted to stay with us at home and was fought tooth and nail. i ended up having to pick up kayla early from school because i was threatened that they would be there first. i couldn't believe that as my husband was on his death bed, i had to deal with my child being taken away from me, too. they actually came into my house and made me feel bad about the situation. i had never been more stunned and numb at the same time. finally, i asked them to leave and not put us through even more stress. tuesday i got a massage, the best therapy that i finally invested in for myself the month that miguel was told he wouldn't make it through winter. miguel's brother had flown in from texas to spend some time with him, so i was able to take this mini break.

but when his brother left on wednesday, miguel started declining even more. the rest of thursday, miguel had an incredibly difficult time getting out of bed. we were recommended to get a hospital bed. the next day, they not only delivered the bed, but several other pieces of equipment that was just not what one would ever expect to see in their house at our age. miguel was craving ice cream that night, and since my mother was always super thoughtful, she brought over five flavors. after about five bites, miguel was full. that was the last 'meal' miguel had. starting saturday, he only asked for water and coke. hospice nurses would come daily to check on him and explain things to me. throughout this entire 17 month battle, i still wanted to know everything whereas he didn't want to know a thing. mind over matter for him, always.

transition

however at this point, miguel was hallucinating on a regular basis. partly due to the fact that he was on an automatic oxycodone drip. every four minutes he set his alarm on his watch just to make sure he was getting the extra dose. i remember when he called me out of the shower one day and as i came to him naked and dripping wet, he got all sheepish. he looked to the side, embarrassed, and said, 'you don't have any clothes on.' i said it was okay, because i was his wife. he said, 'you are? i love you?' and i said, 'yes, i am your wife and you love me.' i had read about how things like this would happen in the end, so as much as it pained me, i understood. i also came to understand that even though we shared many passionate love making experiences together throughout our six years together, that when i had to bathe my husband because he could no longer, that intimacy took a whole new level.

i had many roles during this time frame- wife, mother, caregiver, nurse, etc. miguel actually said i was the nicest one there. he referred to me as the most gentle and kind nurse who took care of him. i had to gently remind him that i was his wife on occasion, but glad that he felt that love. his other brother and mother flew in from honduras that week. it was so nice that amends were made and he and his mother found peace. in fact, in the end, one of miguel's last wishes were to rest in peace. miguel was somewhat of a difficult man and i was so grateful in the end, that even though i had prayed for years for god to soften his heart, it finally did through this trial. not quite what i wanted in terms of the process, but i believe that this was the only thing that could have caused his heart to change.

part of this transformation of body and soul took the form of a mental journey. they say that in the end, most people talk about going somewhere. miguel thought he was a soldier in the war, in a hospital bed, wondering when all of these things attached to him would be taken off and he could leave. he talked about the rebels coming and when he gave me the word that i should grab his boots near the door and bottles of water so we could leave at the drop of a hat. he also claimed that his chapstick was a hot commodity and to not let them have it. we had also watched the entire collection of the sopranos in his last days, so when he would wake up in the middle of the night having spanish monologues for four hours, all i could do is smile. there were light forms of this comic relief that lightened the mood during this difficult time.

one of the funniest moments, if i can say that with a heavy heart, was the day that miguel was put on morphine. the hospice nurse said that most likely he would go into a state of unconsciousness within thirty minutes or so. well, after taking the morphine, miguel would not shut the fuck up. and chatty as hell would be the last phrase used to describe my husband, as he was a man of very few words. he was a funny man, though, and this was a perfect segway to the end. he even joked that his mother should try some of the morphine. right after i administered it, i explained to miguel that one of my friends was dropping off dinner. he asked what was being brought. i told him some

19

sort of gourmet chicken pasta dish. he said 'oh my goodness, i don't think i can wait that long.' (mind you, it had been four days since he had eaten anything.) i was surprised, and actually questioned, 'oh, you want some?' and he said, 'um, of course. i haven't eaten in days!!' anyway, i jumped at that and immediately heated up some baked ziti that another friend had delivered a few days prior and walked in with a plate. he said, 'what is that?' he thought i could hook it up to him like a feeding tube. i explained that we didn't have that capability, but if he wanted some, that he could just eat some. he agreed, and took one bite. he gnawed on it for a bit and after eating one whole noodle, he was exhausted and said he was stuffed. anyway, if you were there, it was funny.

after a couple of hours, i got worried. i actually called the nurse and asked if i did messed up the dosage. don't get me wrong, it was wonderful to see miguel with this much enthusiasm, but i felt like he hadn't talked so much in his entire life. and being that his native tongue was spanish, i didn't understand half of what was coming out. but we were talking. and that was wonderful. this opportunity isn't always given to people. to have closure, to ask the questions, to share, to love and to express it verbally, knowing that your loved one is going to pass soon. i was extremely grateful for these moments and knowing exactly how he wanted things handled in the end. not everyone has this chance to communicate. it was absolutely precious.

the next day he was still chatty and we had some more good times. they say that in the end people get one last burst of energy before they pass. this was it. i had arranged for kayla to spend the weekend with a friend so she wouldn't have to be at home the whole time. miguel told me that he wouldn't make it through the weekend. so that night, kayla read miguel a letter she had written to him and they said their goodbyes. another special moment in life. we slept hard that night, and good thing, as the next would not come so easy.

miguel was having a difficult time relaxing the next day. he had been bed ridden for a week, so we had learned how to move him with sheets and ensure that he had plenty of pillows to keep comfortable. we were running low on the morphine, so when the nurse came in the late afternoon, she told us to go to the pharmacy for a refill. so his brother left to get some. he could not have come back from the pharmacy fast enough. miguel was extremely uncomfortable. the nurse told us that she thought this was the end. we had a few minutes to say goodbye. his lungs were filling up with fluid and that was the immense amount of pressure that he was feeling as we were trying so very hard to get him comfortable.

it was very peaceful in the end, almost mechanical. miguel became unconscious, his eyes closed, and as i was holding his hand, i could feel the warmth leaving his body. his breathing started to slow as his chest did with every breath he took. it seemed like his soul was slowly being extracted from his body each time he exhaled. eventually, no other breath came out. he had died. i shed one tear immediately after he passed. i was relieved. he was no longer suffering or in pain.

after his mother and brother spent a few minutes with him separately, i went into the room with the hospice nurse and helped her prepare his body for cremation. she said that in her thirty years of doing this, i was the only one who had helped afterwards. i just knew that miguel would 'die' to be in that condition and i needed to take care of him immediately. we had already discussed that he wanted to be cremated in one of his torn white t-shirts and his boxer briefs, so that's what i put him in. the hearse pulled up within thirty minutes and took him away. i went for a walk alone around the neighborhood to process what had just happened. my husband had just died. i was a widow at the age of thirty.

eventually i made it back home after wandering around aimlessly. i sat with my mother, his mother and brother. there was nothing to say. there was something that i had to say to the rest of the world though. i had been sending emails throughout this process to several friends of mine and miguel's to keep them in the loop. and knowing for almost a year that i would have to eventually send out an email to disclose the fact that his life had ended was something i needed to do. i cried myself to sleep again that night. the next morning i woke up and began taking all his clothing upstairs for his family to go through. i couldn't look at his things. they needed to go. his pocket watches, his shoes, his jackets, everything. it wasn't that i was trying to forget him, but it was sort of a cleansing for me. it was my way of moving on.

so many people told me how strong i was through this process. i always said i had been praying for it for months. i read a lot online and spoke with all of his doctors. knowledge about what was going to happen helped me process the information. i guess being able to process what was going to happen over time made it somewhat easier to deal with. i talk about death every day now, and i feel like i had time to prepare and accept it and deal with it. it's not like it was unexpected and happened out of nowhere. by all means, i still break down on occasion, just did two days ago, but for the most part, my grieving existed during his battle. when he died, i was ready to put the painful memory of that time behind me.

those two weeks were the most difficult weeks of my life, but also very precious. this was my first experience with death. i told everyone that i grieved for the seventeen months that he battled the disease and when he died, it was a relief. everyone deals with death differently, and i don't think there's a right or wrong way. after going through his things, i left the house for the first time in days. i headed to the mall to find a black dress for his service and felt like a zombie in slow motion walking through packs of people flying by me in the mall. of course i went to banana republic first and broke down in one of my old associates arms. sadly, after scouring the mall for a simple black dress and finding nothing, i went to la rancherita, a place we used to frequent, and had lunch outside by myself. and cried again.

after finishing my meal and tears, i went to the crematorium to get his ashes. i couldn't find a container that fit his personality, so they just put his ashes in five separate boxes, so each of his siblings and mother could have some of him, too. it was very unsettling to see the urns they had- for children, for pets. interesting when you go through something, whatever it is, to get a different perspective. still to this day, i have him in one of his humidors, which i thought was quite fitting considering humidors housed cigars with turned to ashes and all, his final resting place. and since miguel was a big cigar smoker, ever the more fitting the week after his death i actually invited all of his cigar buddies over to the house to select one of his cigars and smoke it in his honor. they passed scotch around and shared stories about miguel while they smoked the cigars.

when i came back home i was feeling better than i had all day. until I walked inside. as soon as i opened the door, i saw several plants and flower arrangements. all of my kitchen countertops were consumed with food and casseroles were erupting out of my refrigerator. i lost my shit. i know that people were trying to show their love and support by sending these things, but it was just a painful reminder to me of all that had transpired. i felt awful, but hope i expressed why i wanted none of this around. his family went outside and let me have the house to myself during this meltdown.

i immediately contacted my best friend and told her to tap into my email and send a message out to everyone to please not send any more things my way. she ended up asking for people to send a donation to the leukemia and lymphoma society in lieu of flowers or meals. within two weeks, over $5,000 had been raised and a team had been formed to walk with me for light the night, a leukemia and lymphoma society fundraiser that honors fighters, survivors, and those we lost to blood cancers. this tradition continues each year.

brand new day

miguel died on a friday, saturday was the blur, and on sunday, we were hosting a memorial service at the house. kayla was supposed to come home an hour or two before the ceremony began. when she came home, she sadly saw what i had upon my arrival back home- flowers, plants, etc. as well as the door to the bedroom open, which had been closed during those last few weeks. i felt awful that i had led her right into the same trap i entered in only a day before. but she knew. we went to her room and cried and talked about everything. we got dressed in our black dresses and headed down to the living room.

friends and family poured in, and we all started sharing stories about miguel. his sister shared hers via skype from france which all brought us from laughter to tears. his brothers both shared stories of how their big brother impacted their lives, also leaving us laughing with tears. i ended the sharing with the story of how we met and how his death was just a part of life. i challenged people to look at their lives- what they were doing with them, where they were going, how they were living, and what happens next. i think that death reminds us to live and how special it is to live each day like it's our last.

after everyone left, kayla asked if she could have something of miguel's so she could remember him by. we went through his bedside drawer and she selected a cigar pipe, one of his lighters, his pocket knife, a handkerchief, a flashlight, a memo book, his blackberry, and a few other random gadgets. her father had a fit when he looked into her book bag and found that she had brought these to school. oops… anyway, it was interesting to see what she wanted to take of his to keep his memory alive. obviously not the typical things for an eight year old to possess, but i wasn't thinking about them being used by her, just the memories that she had of miguel with them.

after a few days, it was time for me to take his mother and brother to the airport. we stopped off at one of his favorite eateries, pho 9n9. after devouring our soups, we got in his car, one of his prides and joys. the tire light came on. i thought this was miguel sending us a message that we had eaten so much that we sank the tires. after i dropped them off at the airport, the oil light came on. i was like, 'really, miguel?' i have a tendency to break things, so i just thought this was funny that his car was now giving me problems. anyway, i ended up selling my car to pay off his, and have since scratched it and dented it here and there due to my carelessness. he'd be rolling in his grave if he wasn't cremated. every time something struck the car i flinch and apologize to him. he was the guy that parked a mile away so no one would accidentally touch it. sorry miguel…

as the days passed, and after making several phone calls to cancel everything in his name and having to recant the phrase that 'my husband died' and that's why i am cancelling this or that, i finally felt like i could move forward. i went back to work at the end of october, heading into the holiday season. my boss quit the friday before black friday, a mortal sin, so this was the seventh time i would be without a store manager. i was told i would never run either of the large stores due to the volume, and the fact that i had never run a store, but when the opportunity to interview came up in january, i jumped at the chance. i thought it was the right team, the right time, etc. instead of getting a call back for a second interview, though, i was called back and told they gave it to someone else. i couldn't believe it.

i called my friend on the way home and he said something that made me think about an idea that i had over a decade ago to have my own boutique. at the time, i thought 'too risky, i don't have any money' fleeting thought gone. and even though i still didn't have any money and it was risky, i realized now that life was short. i loved what i did, but i couldn't do it there anymore. i've always been a 'carpe diem' girl, taking latin for 6 years, but never quite like this.

the next day my daughter and i went to charlotte to visit friends. the friend we were staying with owned her own salon, so i started asking questions on being self-employed. she was having a party that night for people with children, so her neighbors that she had just met only two weeks prior showed up. as we were getting to know one another, i mentioned my current situation and it just so happened that this neighbor did commercial real estate in raleigh and asked if i wanted the specs to brier creek, cameron village, and north hills. coincidence? i think not, yet again...

i came back to work on tuesday and asked to confide in an associate who was working part time at banana but owned her own boutique. she told me that she closed up shop recently and was selling all of her fixtures on friday and would i want them for a fraction of the price that they were worth. wow. on friday i looked inside the 10x10 unit and said 'i'll take it all.'

it was one night that i was attempting to design my business card, that 'the art of style' came to me. this was to be the name of my business. just another heaven sent gift. i always believed that clothing was an expression of who we are as people, and i loved helping people find themselves. so eventually, that became my logo, 'find yourself.' obviously having multiple meanings. i was so excited about this great new venture that i brought a few friends at my after holiday party to my computer to show them my business card design and break the news that i was going to leave banana republic and open a boutique of my own.

it was also in january that i was approached by the leukemia and lymphoma society about fundraising again. they were talking about this man and woman of the year campaign and i explained that of course i was wanting to raise money again, so who were we helping out? they then explained that they were nominating me to run. not quite what i was expecting. this campaign was a competition between men and women to see who could raise the most money in a ten week period of time, and whoever raised the most, won the title of man or woman of the year. so with this commitment and new found desire to escape corporate america, i wrote a business plan in two months, prior to the start of the campaign.

i did a ton of research, got consulted through the process, interviewed successful and not so successful small business owners and wrote my little heart out. everything in my business plan pretty much was written from my experience at banana republic. my purpose, values, and behaviors, target segments, and philosophy were very much like gap, inc, but infused with a little kendra. it was hard to get started, but once i got to writing, it rolled out quite quickly. before i knew it, i was going to the secretary of state to establish my business. it just so happened to be on my 11 year anniversary with banana republic. a short month later, i finished my business plan just in time to devote myself to the campaign.

for ten tiring weeks i diligently worked to raise as much as i could. i had a cigar smoker, in honor of miguel, of course, a beer tasting with local brewers and musician (friends). i was also a celebrity bartender, and had another event at a local lounge. when setting up this event, i had no idea how much my life would be impacted. i was running late, which is incredibly normal for me, but this time i was about three hours behind schedule (that is not so normal). i was actually on the corner of the street when i received a phone call from the same friend who triggered my memory about opening my boutique. he had just seen *wicked* and was going on about how fabulous it was. this was unusual in the respect that this friend is usually in bed around this time getting his beauty rest, so i suggested we meet for a drink.

we went back and forth about where to go, and finally he just said that i should just get my things taken care of and we'd meet up later. so off i went to the space to solidify the event. upon arrival, i saw this gentleman whom i recognized as a client from banana republic but hadn't seen in about five years, but he had grown out his hair. well, after miguel's death, i felt compelled to cut all of mine off. so when i exclaimed, 'hey, i know you! you grew out your hair!' and he said, 'and you cut all yours off!' well, that conversation lasted several hours. who knew a comment about hair would lead to...

light conversation

he had recently been separated and was devastated as anyone would be going through that after a marriage of 18 years. he was beside himself about getting back out into the dating scene. i told him not to even think about dating and worrying about that nonsense. things would unfold and happen naturally and not to force it. well, i gave him my number if he ever wanted to talk and the next day he donated to my campaign and asked his friends via email to help support me as well. that week i had the most online donations, so i was able to bring 10 of my friends to flemings for the mid-point party for the campaign. since he was part of my success, i asked if he wanted to go. he came, and during dinner, it was like my other 9 friends didn't exist. we talked the whole time.

we all decided to go out, and he had taken a cab to get there, so he rode with us downtown and we hung out at a local spot and had drinks. apparently he thought i was interested in someone else in the crowd, so he left with another friend. later, i got a text from him, but didn't know it was him. he asked me to lunch. i didn't think he had a car, cause he had cabbed it the time before, so i offered to come downtown to him. we walked through downtown raleigh and had lunch at a local spot. another wonderful encounter, but really just thought we had good conversation and i certainly wasn't looking for anything. well then we started texting more and had a little flirting here and there.

i went to new york to go to the tradeshow, and was thinking of him, texting him regularly. when i came back, i hosted another event, which he also came to, and after it ended, he kissed me. and for those of you who don't know, kissing is the most important element in creating chemistry with your partner, and needless to say, we were compatible. he flew off to new york the very next day, and said for the first time how much he wanted to leave new york to come back and see me. he came back just in time for the summer charity fashion show.

so now was the main event. we had over 500 people come to the renaissance hotel and had an amazing spread of food, wine, silent, and live auction items. after the live auction, our fabulous auctioneer did a call to arms for a gift of hope. he asked for people to donate just out of the goodness of their heart. maybe they didn't win something they wanted from the live auction or maybe they didn't like anything, but wanted to be able to give back. so in support of me and my effort to raise money for the leukemia and lymphoma society, he started the gift of hope at $1,000. you could hear crickets. however, my newfound boyfriend, who obviously was behind the scenes due to the nature of me doing this campaign in honor of my late husband, made the first bid. my jaw dropped. the bidding then went to $500, and several people gave. then $250, and so many more gave. $100 waves in the audience it seemed. at this point i was in the bathroom balling my eyes out at the generosity of the crowd.

someone had to come and get me because they wanted me to speak after the auction, so i came out and thanked everyone for their support. we kicked off the second half of the show and ended with 'empire state of mind' which was awesome, cause all my friends call me carrie bradshaw. there was a standing ovation and my heart melted. i was so touched and overwhelmed that we had raised $15,000 from the show. all of it was to be matched by gap, inc. and donated to my campaign for woman of the year. so four weeks later, the campaign had come to an end. for ten weeks i had talked to everyone i knew and didn't, about raising awareness and money for the cause. it was all so humbling.

at the man and woman of the year finale there was a video shown from an informational interview that each of the candidates gave at the midpoint party. well, i felt like i must have been a blubbering idiot, cause i wasn't in it. then there i was. it was so interesting. i had told miguel's story a million times. talking was my therapy. but never had i heard my story being told. a completely different scenario. really, like an out of body experience, or maybe that's just what it's like to see yourself on a video. anyway, i lost my shit. i moved myself by hearing what i went through. i know it sounds weird, but i cannot describe it any other way.

after the video aired, they were ready to announce the winners. i was running against doctors and lawyers and presidents of companies, i never thought i had a chance to win this campaign. in fact, most of my events were a bust, but awesome in that they were intimate and special in their own way, with, of course, the exception of the fashion show, which was an incredible success. and that's what did it. as i was wiping the tears off my face from the video shown, it was revealed that i had raised over $30,000 and actually won the campaign. i was in complete disbelief, questioning how me, a manager at banana republic, actually won the campaign. everyone was now asking 'what next?'

well, knowing my intentions, i shared my dreams with confidants, and was working hard on gaining a space and finding vendors. i was patiently waiting for my house to sell (i couldn't afford it financially, but also didn't want to stay there emotionally). about a month after the campaign ended, my house finally sold. i had looked at a place shortly after we found out that miguel wasn't going to 'make it through the winter', but had lost it on contingency after my house didn't sell in the three month window. well, that one house, the only one that was available in the community i wanted, was still available three months later. nope, not a coincidence. so, i bought my house, was supposed to go to the bank to solidify a loan for my store the next day but didn't cause i am a crazy organized nut who had to unpack every box instead and just went into work that friday and put in my notice. the best decision i ever made.

it was kinda funny. i walked in that day, feeling light as a feather. crazy cause i hadn't secured the loan yet, but was taking a giant leap of faith knowing that this was what i was supposed to do. this was my interview day. i loved these days at work. i had 16 interviews, back to back and while i was cramming a sandwich down my throat, my boss asked me a question about where something was. i said 'here or there, but who knows.' then he said, 'well maybe you can answer me this, why did we order a second microwave?' so pause-

two weeks prior, i was ordering supplies for the store. they finally came up with a system that had pictures which was a brilliant concept created by someone in corporate cause ordering supplies for the stores was a complete cluster. well, when i had been transferred to that location a year prior, they didn't have a microwave for their staff. ludicrous. so i brought one from home that i was not using. so when i ordered the microwave with the other supplies, i knew that i would have had my notice put in. well, our supplies dropped on friday instead of monday, so when i was confronted by the question, i handed my boss my letter of resignation. after reading it he looked up and said, 'you're leaving?' and i said 'yes. i'm going to open a boutique of my own.' then he said 'what does this have to do with the microwave?' i said, 'oh, that's mine, and i'm taking it with me when i leave.' awesome.

carpe diem

so on august 1, 2010, i was officially self-employed. my initial spot that i had found for my store backed out the week before i went to milan for a buying trip. i had an oh shit moment, then my boyfriend encouraged me to go across the street. i was trying to do the whole live, work, play thing and the initial spot would have been just a little walk from my house. across the street was a mile and crazy intersection, but i said 'the only place i'd want would be in between starbucks and salon blu and that place doesn't exist.' well guess what. it did. and it was 1200 square feet. and it was available. a.ma.zing.

i had keys within two weeks. it was an old chiropractor's office with blue and green tile, blue carpet, and seafoam green walls. ew. i gave the keys to my contractor on a friday morning and went out of town. when i came back on monday at 3pm, they had ripped everything out, tore down two offices within the space, built two fitting rooms, and were putting the second coat of paint on the walls when i walked in. so i transferred the forty boxes of clothing from my four story town house to the store and started unpacking. kinda cool.

i had several people from banana republic come to help me out. found out that three weeks after i quit, 28 other people had left, too. sad times. it was becoming such a toxic environment at br. also found out the wednesday before my grand opening that friday, that the guy who got the promotion i wanted, got fired. ah justification. so glad i never got that promotion. i would have never done this otherwise. thank you banana republic for all that you taught me. thank you to the leaders who actually led and the countless associates that i interviewed, hired, and trained for all their meaningful lessons that i learned while being a servant leader during my 11 and a half years at banana republic. i am eternally grateful for all the many things that i learned over the decade that i slaved away there, but am so happy that i am no longer there. all i really miss is the people. and the hugs. i used to get like 50 hugs a day from clients.

i'm working up to that number with my clients now. i absolutely love what i do. i love people, am addicted to clothing, and enjoy traveling. can't remember if i mentioned that yet. i love the fact that every day is different and exciting and new and i meet new fabulous people that come into my store every day. and several now have become friends which i love dearly. and who doesn't love ordering everything for your store and keeping one for thyself?! now i feel the need to get rid of my thirty banana republic suits…

anyway, i opened my store on november 2, 2010. i was super sick, running a fever and had gotten a speeding ticket the night before as i was heading to the grocery store to buy food and drinks for the grand opening party. unfortunately it was closed by the time the cop was through with me, so i had to wake up extra early to go to the store in the freezing rain with a fever. ugh. don't you just hate those days? but, by the end of the day, it was so worth it. i had close to 100 people show up for the grand opening to show their support and thank goodness, cause my leap of faith caused my bank account to be very slim by then. however the first day confirmed that all would be well.

and well it was. and well, it was hard. being a small business owner was a challenge. is a challenge. and i thought that i would be bored. i was used to seeing a couple hundred people an hour at banana republic. now i might see a few people in a day. but bored, i was not. there was so much to do and so many exciting things to think about and create and plan and do. i was a merchant for the first half of my life at banana republic so i learned how to make things visually stimulating. cause when you do that people get attracted to it and go mess it up. i learned how to create a compelling experience with clothing, color, layering, implementing wardrobing and impact fixtures and concoct displays that command attention. retail is the balance of merchandising with the customer experience. and that is what means the most to me. that each and every client who walks through my doors has an amazing experience. that all of their senses delighted- through touch, sight, sound, smell, and feeling- all are relevant.

most clients that enter my store comment on how lovely it smells (a vanilla glade plug in), the music we play is alternative, but not excluding, volume is balanced so one can enjoy the music, but have a conversation at the same time. people say that they feel comfortable in my store. it is a very welcoming environment with the lighting as well as the furniture. i have had many good conversations and cries with complete strangers on my loveseat. the way the clothing is displayed is clean and easy to navigate through, as not to be overwhelming. i describe it as a lifestyle approach, which is what i think style and clothing signifies. i have clients that range from 17 to 70. my style is very clean, classic, modern, current, sophisticated, sexy, and edgy. sorry, my personality is multifaceted, and my store reflects just that…

the second half of my life at br was all about the customer experience. so i did everything dealing with the internal and external client. and i love my peeps. so i was in heaven. doing my own thing. the first two months were great. both my merchant and my cpa were surprised at how well i was doing. obviously i was new and it was the holiday season, but truly, there is an invisible forcefield around my store. you'd think being connected to starbucks that i'd be slammed, but no one knows that i exist. i think that's why i have a lot of international clients and others from larger cities, cause they are looking for something to do or go and locals stick to routines. i keep joking with my starbucks about knocking down the wall in between their store and mine and that i'll franchise with them if they really want to...

so, in january, i met my cpa who said numbers don't lie, people make numbers lie. hired. i am an unrealistic optimist. my cup is always overflowing and everything is always seen through my rose colored glasses. i will always see the best things in everyone and every situation to a fault, i'm told. it's not that i'm ignorant to the nastiness of the world, i just choose to look for the good. anyway, since i live in my fantasy world, i need a realist to take care of my books and finances. speaking of my fantasy world, i had the most amazing daughter on the planet and was in the best relationship with a gorgeous man who was just as stunning on the inside. i had never been so happy.

making it happen

so the months passed, business kept moving forward. except in the j
months. j months suck, by the way. january, june, and july. ya'll need to
make a conscious effort to come shopping in those months, k... well,
since i hired my cpa in january, we were already behind. so he did a lot
of back work and redid my taxes, well, supposed to. in june, we were to
have our huge recap of all the business stuff for the first time, so i was
anxiously awaiting this meeting. i had been flying blind the whole time.
still can't tell if that's the leap of faith turned into flight or not...

my cpa called me to see if we could reschedule our meeting cause he
had just had unexpected knee surgery, due to a soccer jury. two weeks
had gone by and i hadn't heard anything, so i reached out and left a
message. another week went by so i left another. the third week i got
a letter from the irs so i called yet again. the gentleman that answered
the phone said, 'oh, you must not have heard. he died.' my cpa had
an aneurysm and collapsed a few days after we spoke. obviously
nothing else matters when you hear news such as that, so my problems
became insignificant.

but after another three weeks went by, we were heading into august and i still had not had my reality check. so i called the firm and they passed me onto the other firm who took over all the accounts. during our initial meeting, i knew that this would not be a good fit, but wanted to get some kind of information from them before moving on. i'm a pretty faced paced, high energy person and they were just not operating on my same frequency, in addition they hated trees (wanted paper everything). however, when they didn't show for our next meeting i was livid. partially because i was up sick all night the night before and woken up early to come in extra early for our meeting. grrrrrr....

so i simply just asked for them to send me the files cause i had found someone else to take care of my accounting. well the information came across and nothing was there. on october 19, i found out that none of my bookkeeping had been completed, nor had my taxes been redone the year miguel died. so basically i paid for services not rendered. it was also on this day that i spent over three hours on the phone with the irs and the nc dept of revenue only to find that all of my sales tax had been filed underneath the wrong ein (apparently i was some company in nevada). joy.

after work that day, i had a speaking engagement at nc state university. after i spoke, i had about seven people asking to be my intern and when was i going to open shop in downtown raleigh. well, one thing i forgot to mention is that i was actually in the process of opening a wine bar. where i live in brier creek, there is no such thing as nightlife, so my whole live, work, play was lacking in the play category. it was to be called the lounge, a wine bar, specializing in cocktails and corresponding mocktails and fine scotches and whiskey. anyway, after finding out about all my bookkeeping or lack thereof, i told my boyfriend that night that i think i'm just to stick to what i know best and open another store. he agreed.

so when i woke up at 4 o'clock in the morning and couldn't sleep because i was so excited, i got up and started emailing people about leasing in cameron village. the woman in charge had been on vacation in italy and it would not be until monday that she returned. and we all know that when you're on vacation, coming back to work is a nightmare. wanting to tread the fine line of being persistent without being annoying, but time was of the essence. it was nearing the end of october and if I wasn't going to be open for the holidays, there really would be no point of opening at all.

but through balancing my aggressiveness with my charm, i was able to get her to come and meet me at my store that friday. by the following friday i had keys. we celebrated our year anniversary of our brier creek location and a week later on 11.11.11 we opened the second location. so as i am writing this memoir, i am pushing my deadline of 12.12.12 as the release date of my book. as my daughter said it was the last really cool date that I had to do something great. so thanks be to her for giving me the great idea and just a little bit of pressure to accomplish this next goal of mine. funny how i found out from a client that november is national novel writing month. not that this is a large publication, but still. neat that i just happen to be writing the majority of this in the month of november. breaching 15,000 words!

and another wonderful happening, a few weeks ago a client of mine told me that he had just self-published on kindle. my mind was blown. you can self-publish?! well then, this unrealistic goal just might be achievable, considering that i only have 5 more days to do it. in fact, i was never planning on writing a book. over a year ago i spoke for a major attorney in the area. at the time, i was on track to open my wine bar. so when we were discussing the bullet points of my story that i'd be sharing with his presidential group, he said, 'so when you write your book.' and i said, 'oh, i'm not writing a book.' and he said, 'so when you write your book.' and i was like, 'i think you must have me confused with someone else. i'm not writing a book.' and that's when he said, 'you should write a book.' and then i got it. i could write a fucking book. so thanks be to you sir for giving me this great idea to begin with.

so what they say of having two locations is so true. a good idea in theory, but it's not double the issues, it's quadruple them. so when i opened my first location, i was only open from 10am-6pm tuesday through saturday for quality of life. i don't believe we were meant to work our lives away. of course i had been there at 10 o'clock at night or 7:30 in the morning for clients, but wanted to give myself time to enjoy life. well, when i opened the store in cameron village, they mandated that i be open seven days a week. so i went from five days a week, to seven days a week times two. this is where i tell people i lost my brain.

i made it through nine months of this, barely, but was able to convince management at cameron village to let me take sunday and monday off my hours of operation. i still do by appointment, but this also permits me much needed peace. i also do private wardrobe consulting, so this also allows me to have a bit of flexibility. but none of this would have ever been possible without my natalie. i managed natalie at banana republic for over three years. after opening my first location, she asked if she could intern with me. after i opened the second store, she managed that location. she is so incredibly talented. not only as a designer herself, but as a social media megamind, the most incredible stylist, customer service specialist, courageous cheese ball, eloquent writer, and loyal individual. thanks be to you natalie for all that you have done over the past two years. your friendship and dependability have allowed me to chase my dreams and without you, none of this would have happened. i will always be in debt to you.

find yourself

so as we head into the end of yet another year of life, i guess i'd just like to take this opportunity to share with you my story. we all have one and you only live once. take the time you have here on earth to do whatever it is that makes you happy. i believe we all have god given talents and the best way to say thanks is to use them and share them with others. there is a reason that there's a saying that if you do what makes you passionate, you'll never work a day in your life.

i just spoke for the career fair at my daughter's school not too long ago. and my message to these 13 and 14 year olds was that one day, we will all die. it is a fact of life. we tend to not think about our mortality. we think what we'll be doing tomorrow, or next week, or next month, or next year. well, we're not vampires, as much as i'd like to be one. i could get in a car accident later this afternoon and die instantaneously, or i could battle cancer and die slowly for seventeen months. either way, it's going to happen to all of us. point being, do what you want to do. if you don't want to be a doctor or lawyer, but your parents are pushing you in that direction, be open minded and listen, but they had that opportunity to do that for themselves. this is your one life to live. don't live for someone else's dreams. you have your own to chase. and no one is going to do them for you. you have to find a way to make it happen. and money does not buy happiness. not that i have any, but i can tell you, i've never been so broke and happy in my life. i'm doing what i love and helping others along the way, and that is priceless.

one of the best things about working at banana republic was learning how to have difficult conversations. thanks be to one of the most brilliant men i have ever met as well as the best leader to have ever worked for. i have this stupid little zipper analogy that i used to share with my associates. imagine that my zipper is down. obviously, i have no clue that i am walking around exposing myself. i would never want to be in this situation, as it's embarrassing. well, clearly i am unaware of my flaw. and if everyone else notices it, but never says anything, my zipper will remain down. however, if someone has the guts to tell me that my zipper is down, i'll pull it up. and if i keep hearing that my zipper is down from several individuals it becomes a consistent pattern of behavior, a problem. well, i can take that feedback and do nothing, maybe i want to walk around with my zipper down. but more than likely, i want to be the best that i can be, so i will, after hearing this feedback, hopefully start double checking myself on a regular basis to make sure my zipper is up. i know that may seem like a silly example, but i take that to every aspect of my life.

typically we don't know our flaws unless they're pointed out to us. i mean our parents, lovers, and friends tend to sing our graces, right? my point is, is that unless someone has the courage to come up and talk to me about my problem, my problem will never be fixed. if everyone notices my problem and just talks about it amongst themselves, then everyone else can just participate in allowing my flaw to exist. as much as i have intuition and would love to be a mind reader, i'm not. nor are most people. so if you're having a problem with someone- your lover, your daughter, your friend, your coworker, your doctor, tell them, and do it with love. it's never what we say, it's how we say it, but if we never speak, no one knows, and then it tends to build up. in any relationship, it's always the small things. the big things you can't ignore. but if you communicate calmly to articulate how you feel when xyz happened, i promise it can only help. and by all means, i continue to put my foot in my mouth, but i can tell you that i have a certain peace in my life for sharing honest feelings with the individuals in my life.

and most importantly, relationships- all of them- are built on a foundation of trust. without it, you have nothing. my marriage was only a little over a year, and the whole time miguel was sick, so i know i don't have much to compare. but my method of thought is that marriage is a partnership. that is your partner for life. you want your partner to want to be with you, not forced. and vice versa. life is short, as long as it may seem. but it can be good and wonderful, but you are ultimately in charge of that. you can make a conscious effort to 'fix' something for yourself or someone else. none of us are perfect. we all have flaws. i believe that's what keeps us humble. i also believe that bad things happen to help make us appreciate all the good things that much more. and that everything, everything happens for a reason.

it's a mindset, a way of life. enjoy yours and share yourself with others. and in the process you will find yourself more fulfilled and contributing to being the positive change you want to see in the world. thank you for taking your time to read this and i hope you find yourself soon. but know that if you need help, i'm here...

Printed in the United States
by Baker & Taylor Publisher Services